BODY *of* PROOF

A Study on the Resurrection of Jesus

JEREMIAH J. JOHNSTON

Lifeway Press®
Brentwood, Tennessee

EDITORIAL TEAM

Jeremiah J. Johnston
Writer

Reid Patton
Senior Editor

Stephanie Cross
Associate Editor

Denise Wells
Graphic Designer

Tyler Quillet
Managing Editor

Joel Polk
Publisher, Small Group Publishing

John Paul Basham
Director, Adult Ministry Publishing

Published by Lifeway Press® • © 2023 Jeremiah J. Johnston

No part of this book may be reproduced or transmitted in any form or by any means, electronic or mechanical, including photocopying and recording, or by any information storage or retrieval system, except as may be expressly permitted in writing by the publisher. Requests for permission should be addressed in writing to Lifeway Press®; 200 Powell Place, Suite 100; Brentwood, TN 37027-7707.

ISBN 978-1-4300-9278-0 • Item 005847234

Dewey decimal classification: 232.97
Subject headings: JESUS CHRIST--RESURRECTION \ HOPE \ CHRISTIANITY

Author Photo by Cameron Bertuzzi

To order additional copies of this resource, write to Lifeway Resources Customer Service; 200 Powell Place, Suite 100; Brentwood, TN 37027-7707; fax 615-251-5933; call toll free 800-458-2772; order online at lifeway.com; email orderentry@lifeway.com.

Printed in the United States of America

Adult Ministry Publishing • Lifeway Resources
200 Powell Place, Suite 100 • Brentwood, TN 37027-7707

Contents

About the Author

Jeremiah J. Johnston, PhD, is a New Testament scholar, pastor, author, Bible teacher, and apologist, and he ministers internationally as president of Christian Thinkers Society (ChristianThinkers.com). Jeremiah loves the local church and serves as pastor of apologetics and cultural engagement at Prestonwood Baptist Church as well as dean of spiritual development at Prestonwood Christian Academy. Jeremiah is also the Senior Fellow for Christian Origins at the Institute for Global Leadership at Dallas Baptist University. His passion is working with churches, pastors, and students in equipping Christians to give intellectually informed reasons for what they believe.

Jeremiah has distinguished himself speaking in churches of all denominations and has authored articles in both popular magazines and scholarly books, journals, and media programs. As a theologian who has the unique ability to connect with people of all ages, and as a culture expert, he has been interviewed numerous times and has reviewed and contributed articles across a spectrum of national shows and podcasts

As a New Testament scholar, Johnston has published with Oxford University Press, E. J. Brill, Bloomsbury T & T Clark, Macmillan, and Mohr Siebeck. He completed his doctoral residency in Oxford in collaboration with Oxford Centre for Missions Studies and received his PhD from Middlesex University (UK). He has also earned advanced degrees in theology from Acadia University and Midwestern Baptist Theological Seminary. Jeremiah is married to Audrey, and they are parents to five children—Lily Faith, Justin, and triplets: Abel, Ryder, and Jaxson.

How to Use this Study

Body of Proof: A Study on the Resurrection of Jesus provides four lessons that can be used for group or personal Bible study. Each session includes a group study along with five days of personal study to use throughout the week. In order to have the best experience, allow forty-five to sixty minutes for the group sessions.

Group Study

Each week of study begins with a group study experience featuring videos filmed on location in Israel. Each experience contains four elements: "Start," "Watch," "Discuss," and "About the Location." The group study gives real, immediately practical teaching to help participants connect the truth and hope of the resurrection to their lives.

START. Each study begins with an introduction to the lesson to come. This section is designed to introduce the week's topic and get the conversation going. Read this section and answer the introductory questions together if you're in a group.

WATCH. This space provides Jeremiah's teaching outline as well as blank space to take notes as you watch the video teaching. Codes to access the teaching videos are included with your purchase of this book and can be found on the insert located at the back of this book. You may watch these videos together as a group of prior to the group meeting.

ABOUT THIS LOCATION. This section gives additional details and resources about the wonderful locations where this study was filmed. Each includes a photo, key biblical text that took place there, brief information, and a QR code that will take participants to a short video with more information from Jeremiah.

DISCUSS. This section is the primary group experience each week. Leaders should spend the majority of the group session teaching while using the verses and questions provided in this section. These sections have three subsections: Read, Apply, and Close.

Personal Study

Each week of the study the personal study examines four reason that we can trust in the truth of the resurrection and place our hope in Jesus.

Week 1

Jesus Predicted His Death and Resurrection

Week 2

Jesus Demonstrated Resurrection Power

Week 3

The Resurrection Makes Sense of our Suffering

Week 4

The Resurrection is the Foundation of our Hope

After attending the group session, members should complete the five days of personal study at home before the next group session. Through this personal study, group members will explore biblical content and application that support the concepts introduced in the video teaching.

Additional Resources

Also available at lifeway.com/bodyofproof you will find a church campaign kit to assist you in making this study a church wide initiative leading into or out of the Easter season. Here you will find: leader's guides for each session, kids and student lessons, family activities, promotional assets, and a church planning guide.

Tips for Leading
a Small Group

Follow these guidelines to prepare for each session.

Prayerfully Prepare

Review. Review the personal studies and group questions ahead of time.

Pray. Be intentional about praying for each person in the group. Ask the Holy Spirit to work through you and the group discussion as you point to Jesus each week through God's Word.

Minimize Distractions

Create a comfortable environment. If group members are uncomfortable, they'll be distracted and therefore not engaged in the group experience. Plan ahead by considering these details:

Seating	Temperature	Lighting
Food or Drink	Surrounding Noise	General Cleanliness

At best, thoughtfulness and hospitality show guests and group members they're welcome and valued in whatever environment you choose to gather. At worst, people may never notice your effort, but they're also not distracted. Do everything in your ability to help people focus on what's most important: connecting with God, with the Bible, and with one another.

Include Others

Your goal is to foster a community in which people are welcome just as they are but encouraged to grow spiritually. Always be aware of opportunities to include any people who visit the group and to invite new people to join your group. An inexpensive way to make first-time guests feel welcome or to invite someone to get involved is to give them their own copies of this Bible study book.

Encourage Discussion

A good small group experience has the following characteristics:

Everyone Participates. Encourage everyone to ask questions, share responses, or read aloud.

No One Dominates—Not Even the Leader. Be sure that your time speaking as a leader takes up less than half of your time together as a group. Politely guide discussion if anyone dominates.

Nobody Is Rushed Through Questions. Don't feel that a moment of silence is a bad thing. People often need time to think about their responses or to gain courage to share what God is stirring in their hearts.

Input Is Affirmed and Followed Up. Make sure you point out something true or helpful in a response. Don't just move on. Build community with follow-up questions, asking how other people have experienced similar things or how a truth has shaped their understanding of God and the Scripture you're studying. People are less likely to speak up if they fear that you don't actually want to hear their answers or that you're looking for only a certain answer.

God and His Word Are Central. Opinions and experiences can be helpful, but God has given us the truth. Trust God's Word to be the authority and God's Spirit to work in people's lives. You can't change anyone, but God can. Continually point people to the Word and to active steps of faith.

Keep Connecting

Think of ways to connect with group members during the week. Participation during the group session is always improved when members spend time connecting with one another outside the group sessions. The more people are comfortable with and involved in one another's lives, the more they'll look forward to being together. When people move beyond being friendly to truly being friends who form a community, they come to each session eager to engage instead of merely attending.

When possible, build deeper friendships by planning or spontaneously inviting group members to join you outside your regularly scheduled group time for activities, meals, group hangouts, or projects around your home, church, or community.

Why Study the Resurrection?

Jesus's resurrection is a central focus of our New Testament Scripture with over three hundred verses referencing this truth. When we study what the Bible teaches about the resurrection of Jesus, we are struck by the power this singular historical event had on the early followers of Jesus. We can also recognize the explosive growth of the church as they spread the gospel, or "good news" of Jesus's resurrection, throughout the world. When we open the Scriptures, we see that belief in bodily resurrection empowered the early church to "[turn] the world upside down" (Acts 17:6); that resurrection faith was the key to their ethics (1 Corinthians 15:58–16:1); that resurrection faith brought hope in moments of worldly despair (2 Corinthians 1); and that resurrection faith caused the earliest followers of Jesus to become the greatest force for God on earth (Galatians 3:28).

The overpowering truth of Jesus's resurrection is the promise of a glorified resurrected body, so make the most of each day, because everything we do today matters for the kingdom of God. In fact, deathlessness is the main descriptor of our future resurrection bodies—they cannot die. They will be physical bodies, not spirit-ghosts or apparitions. We know this because Paul told the church at Philippi that Christ would "transform the body of our humble condition into the likeness of his glorious body" (Philippians 3:21). Christ was raised in a physical body, and Scripture tells us our resurrection bodies will be patterned after His body. Jesus also told His disciples, "Look at my hands and my feet, that it is I myself! Touch me and see, because a ghost does not have flesh and bones as you can see I have" (Luke 24:39).

Despite this, many of today's churches rarely preach series on Jesus's resurrection. Outside of a funeral or Easter service, believers may go weeks or even months without learning about or considering His resurrection. Yet this event is unquestionably at the very center of the New Testament proclamation. Paul stated that, apart from this event, the very faith of his hearers was vain and they were still trapped in sin (1 Corinthians 15:17). How often do believers today hear challenging words such as these?

The gospel teaching and the apologetic significance of Jesus's resurrection are probably the most common applications regarding Jesus's resurrection. However, few of the current books cover the idea that the resurrection of Jesus is also connected to nearly every major theological doctrine as well as many practical areas of Christian living. So, having a weak understanding of the implications of Jesus's resurrection keeps Christians from living fully in Spirit-filled power. First Peter 1:3 serves as a much-needed reminder and promise for every believer today, "Blessed be the God and Father of our Lord Jesus Christ. Because of his great mercy he has given us new birth into a living hope through the resurrection of Jesus Christ from the dead."

The first-generation Christians became unstoppable witnesses for Christ, because they saw Jesus physically alive after a heinous Roman execution. This in depth Bible study will equip you with practical applications and transformational truths to help you live in light of the reality of Jesus's resurrection today. Our study also anticipates modern critics, who are very similar to Jesus's critics. Jesus's critics then demanded evidence. They essentially—and rightly—said, "Well, if you're this person you claim to be, show us a sign." And Jesus responded, "I will give you one sign: my resurrection from the dead" (see Matthew 12:38–42).

The bottom line is this: If Jesus did not rise from the dead, that makes Him a false prophet unworthy of our allegiance, and no rational person should follow Him. But if Jesus did rise from the dead, it seems that He did so in confirmation of His personal and radical claims. And the implications of that truth, that Jesus is alive forevermore, makes us stop and consider, wrap ourselves in the truth of Jesus's resurrection. That is exactly what happened to the first Christians, and we pray this will also be your experience through the truths you learn and apply through this study.

Replacing My "If Onlys" with "If Jesus"

Start

Welcome to Session 1 of Body of Proof.
Use this section to get the conversation started.

What is a belief that you hold with certainty? What gives
you certainty?

How does certainty in something give you hope?

The Gospel writer, Luke, opens his book telling his audience why he wrote it:
"so that you may know the certainty of the things about which you have been
instructed" (Luke 1:4). The goal of this study provide you certainty in the hope of
the resurrection.

Christianity is true, and you can confirm the truth of Christianity by appealing
to what actually happened in history. As we learn in our study together, the power
of the truth of the resurrection results in a fusion of facts and faith. The result is
certainty and confidence to live with hope in Christ today.

This study will journey to different resurrection sites throughout Israel
and help us think through the hope the resurrection brings to our daily lives.
We will begin in Bethany, where Jesus raised Lazarus from the dead. Because He
raised Lazarus, we can trust that He has the power to raise us physically as well
as spiritually.

Pray together before watching this week's video teaching.

Watch

Use this section to take notes and follow the video teaching.

Central Truth

A. I must replace all my "if onlys" with "if Jesus."

B. I will live by "if Jesus," not "if only."

The Tomb of Lazarus in Bethany

Key Texts: John 11:1-55; Mark 14:3-9; Luke 10:3-42; 24:50–53

Lazarus's tomb is located in a first century cemetery and could be the actual tomb. The tomb has been recognized as such since the early fourth century. Given the continuity of village memory, we can be certain that this is the actual tomb or at least the right spot.

For more on Bethany view the video at this QR Code.

Discuss

Use this section to discuss the video teaching.

READ

Resurrection is not an abstract belief or just another fact of history but a person—Jesus Christ. After the death of her brother Lazarus, Jesus stood in front of Martha, urging her to make the leap of faith and place her hope in Him. He challenged her to trust in His resurrection power and exchange her "if only" for an "if Jesus."

Read John 11:1–44 together.

What does it mean that Jesus is the resurrection and the life?

Why did Jesus take the time to ask Martha the question, "do you believe this" (v. 26)?

Why is it important for each of us to answer this question for ourselves?

Jesus raising Lazarus from the dead demonstrates that His claims about being resurrection is life. In this encounter, Jesus interrupted the physical death of Lazarus and showed that He has interrupted spiritual death for all who place their hope in Him—for those who turn their if onlys to if Jesus. From this story we see several immediate applications to our faith.

APPLY

1. Even the closest friends of Jesus experience pain and adversity (vv. 1-5)

How does this encounter confirm that pain is not the end of our story?

2. Jesus is resourceful because He is the source (v. 3).

What are some ways provides for us that build our faith and trust in Him?

3. Instead of being stuck in the past, Jesus wants us to look to the future (vv. 9-10).

What do you have to look forward to because of the certainty of resurrection with Jesus?

4. The Christian lives and dies in hope; death is now no more than sleep, and there is nothing to fear (v. 11).

Why should Jesus's power in this encounter free us from fear? How are sadness and hurt different than fear?

How does Jesus meet those needs as well?

5. Faith trusts God through uncertainty (v. 16).

Why is uncertainty so destabilizing? When our life feels destabilized, why is it essential to have certainty in Jesus?

6. Faith is not what I feel; faith is what I believe (v. 25).

How can our feelings deceive us?

Where are you trusting your belief in Jesus beyond your feelings?

CLOSE

Which of your *if onlys* do you need to replace with an *if Jesus*?

Faith is taking God at His Word and acting accordingly. Our relationship with Jesus Christ is not based on feelings but on faith, which is based on the facts of Scripture. Each week, our personal study will be devoted to investigating one reason we can have certainty in Jesus. This week we'll investigate the truth that "Jesus called it." In other words, Jesus kept His mission front and center with His disciples and early followers—constantly reminding them that He would die and rise on the third day.

Close in prayer and remind the group to complete the five days of personal study.

I Can Trust the
Resurrection Because:

Jesus Called It

DAY 1

Jesus Defies Expectation

KEY SCRIPTURE
Mark 8:29-33

Any parent, grandparent, aunt, or uncle, can probably relate with having to repeat exciting announcements to children. They usually say something like, "Wait, what?" or "Seriously?" Whether because of disbelief or unfamiliarity, they need to be told more than once. Or if you have coached a team, maybe you've said something like, "It'll be worth it in the end," to encourage the players to trust you and the process. Athletes must be reminded of where they are and the goal and then adjust their expectations. Jesus's disciples were no different. They suffered from a brand of disbelieving faith and wrong expectations, and they misunderstood what the real Messiah and true Messianic mission looked like. So, Jesus had to speak very pointedly—and they did not like it.

> Have you been in a training or coaching situation where you didn't get it and needed help? What did you learn from that experience?

We read about the disciples misunderstanding in the Gospel of Mark 8:29 when Jesus asked them, "Who do you say that I am?" (v. 29).

And in response, Peter made a remarkable confession, boldly proclaiming Jesus as the long-awaited Messiah. Yet, what kind of Messiah would Jesus be? Jesus had been hinting at all His messianic mission would entail, but the disciples still didn't understand. They expected a conqueror, not a sufferer. Jesus didn't wait to explain; He took the teaching opportunity.

> *Then he began to teach them that it was necessary for the Son of Man to suffer many things and be rejected by the elders, chief priests, and scribes, be killed, and rise after three days. He spoke openly about this. Peter took him aside and began to rebuke him. But turning around and looking at his disciples, he rebuked Peter and said, "Get behind me, Satan! You are not thinking about God's concerns but human concerns."*

> MARK 8:31-33

At first, Peter got it right. But Peter went from proclaiming Jesus the Messiah to being called "Satan" and being told to get back in line just a few minutes later. Can you relate? We can get things right in our faith, and then have the rug pulled out from us when we misapply what we get right. This is why context is so helpful when we study Scripture. When I open the Bible I always use the CIA method: Context + Interpretation = Application.

Did you know the Gospels record less than one month of Jesus's life? In fact, we only have snippets, or parts, of around twenty-four to twenty-six days of the earthly life of Jesus. In God's plan, we didn't need more than a month of Jesus's life recorded for the power of the gospel to be unleashed and mankind to be rescued. As we open our Bible study this week, the most important aspect of the Gospels is the intentional focus on the final eight days of Jesus's earthly ministry. This final week or so of Jesus's life is referred to by many as "The Passion of the Christ."

Hearing this descriptor may be confusing to some. Why do so many people refer to Jesus's suffering, death, and resurrection as "the passion"? The term "passion" is connected to the Latin word *passiō*, which means suffering. Throughout the Gospels, we see Jesus resetting the disciples' (and our) expectations about what kind of Messiah He would be. These predictions were meant to lead the first disciples and disciples today to realize Jesus is who He claimed to be. Because Jesus is who He claimed to be we can look to Him with confidence and hope.

Read the following passages and as you close today's study, ask the Lord to reveal to you why Jesus had to suffer first and not conquer. Summarize what you learn.

Acts 1:3; 3:18

Luke 17:25; 22:15

Hebrews 13:12

1 Peter 1:21; 3:18; 4:1

Philippians 1:29

DAY 2

Messianic Prophecy and Passion Predictions Are Linked!

KEY SCRIPTURE

Daniel 7:13-14

At the core of Jesus's passion predictions lie three main components:

- In Jerusalem Jesus would suffer and die.

- Jesus would be comprehensively rejected.

- He would be resurrected victoriously "after three days" (Matthew 27:63; Mark 8:31; 9:31; 10:34) or "on the third day" (Matthew 17:23; 20:19; Luke 18:33; 24:7).

Where have you identified these components in your own Bible reading?

Jesus's passion predictions are the climactic tipping point of the Gospels. But the passion was not just predicted in the Gospels, the predictions began in the Old Testament. To quote a great twentieth-century scholar, "Jesus found himself in the Old Testament."[1] The whole cannon of Scripture predicts and proclaims the resurrection.

To what extent have you relied on the Old Testament for information about Jesus's suffering, death and resurrection?

Why is the Old Testament important for understanding the New Testament?

When we read the Old Testament, the Messiah is not a side-bar issue but the focal point. Jesus relied on the Old Testament to clarify His mission and ministry. Because of this we know the cross was not an accident or triumph of evil; it was the preordained will of God, and it was foretold in the Old Testament. Jesus saw Himself as fulfilling Old Testament prophecies. Jesus quoted or alluded to Deuteronomy around fifteen or sixteen times, Isaiah around forty times, and the Psalms around thirteen times.

Jesus's favorite way of referring to himself was the phrase "Son of Man," and this self-designation appears over eighty times in the Gospels. This title also appears in Daniel 7:13–14:

> *I continued watching in the night visions,*
> *and suddenly one like a son of man*
> *was coming with the clouds of heaven.*
> *He approached the Ancient of Days*
> *and was escorted before him.*
> *He was given dominion*
> *and glory and a kingdom,*
> *so that those of every people,*
> *nation, and language*
> *should serve him.*
> *His dominion is an everlasting dominion*
> *that will not pass away,*
> *and his kingdom is one*
> *that will not be destroyed.*
>
> DANIEL 7:13-14

What does this Old Testament passage teach us about Jesus?

How should it build our faith to know that Jesus's life, death, and resurrection were predicted before His earthly ministry began?

DAY 3

The Importance of Jesus's Passion and Resurrection Promises

KEY SCRIPTURES
Mark 8:31; 9:31; 10:33-34; Luke 24

This week we've been looking into predictions about Jesus's life, death, and resurrection. Why are these predictions so important to the fulfillment of the gospel?

Jesus often predicted His violent death. Read the following passage and make note of the repeated ideas and phrases.

> *Then he began to teach them that it was necessary for the Son of Man to suffer many things and be rejected by the elders, chief priests, and scribes, be killed, and rise after three days.*
>
> MARK 8:31

> *For he was teaching his disciples and telling them, "The Son of Man is going to be betrayed into the hands of men. They will kill him, and after he is killed, he will rise three days later."*
>
> MARK 9:31

> *"See, we are going up to Jerusalem. The Son of Man will be handed over to the chief priests and the scribes, and they will condemn him to death. Then they will hand him over to the Gentiles, and they will mock him, spit on him, flog him, and kill him, and he will rise after three days."*
>
> MARK 10:33–34

What repeated themes did you notice?

If the early church had a hashtag or slogan, it would have been #onthethirdday. These words were critical for the earliest witnesses of the resurrection (Acts 10:40; 1 Corinthians 15:4). In the eighth century BC, the Israelite prophet Hosea had used those words to console a defeated Northern Kingdom with the promise that God would restore the nation. Then anticipating the eventual restoration of sinful Israel, he uttered a startling prediction: "He will revive us after two days, and on the third day he will raise us up so we can live in his presence" (Hosea 6:2).

This is one of the most important Bible texts for understanding the interpretation and self-understanding of Jesus because it lies behind His passion predictions. As I've written:

> We hear [Hosea's] prophecy echoed in Jesus' predictions of suffering: "The Son of Man will be delivered into the hands of men, and they will kill him; and when he is killed, after three days he will rise" (Mark 9:31; compare Mark 8:31; 10:33–34). Indeed, the resurrected Jesus himself alludes to Hosea's prophecy: "Thus it is written, that the Christ should suffer and on the third day rise from the dead" (Luke 24:46).[2]

Matthew, Mark, and Luke significantly emphasize Jesus's passion predictions using "on the third day" or "after three days" again and again. Jesus took Hosea 6:1–3 and applied these passages to Himself. The risen Jesus taught more than once from Hosea in discussion with the disciples on the road to Emmaus (Luke 24:13–27) and during another appearance (Luke 24:44–49, specifically verse 46). Without a doubt, this is why Paul calls the gospel the "most important" (1 Corinthians 15:3-4) thing he received.

Why does it matter that Jesus predicted that He would rise from the dead?

Why does it matter that the whole biblical storyline points do and explains the importance of Jesus's resurrection?

DAY 4

A Proclamation of Jesus's Continuing Ministry

KEY SCRIPTURES
Matthew 26:26–29; Mark 14:22–25; Luke 22:14–20

Predictions are fascinating, and when they come true, they're compelling. History remembers well the guarantees of Babe Ruth, Joe Namath, and Muhammad Ali. Skeptics wonder if Jesus really knew what He was doing. And the truth is, yes, Jesus knew exactly what He was doing. He predicted His victory too.

> *As they were eating, Jesus took bread, blessed and broke it, gave it to the disciples, and said, "Take and eat it; this is my body." Then he took a cup, and after giving thanks, he gave it to them and said, "Drink from it, all of you. For this is my blood of the covenant, which is poured out for many for the forgiveness of sins. But I tell you, I will not drink from this fruit of the vine from now on until that day when I drink it new with you in my Father's kingdom."*

> MATTHEW 26:26–29

What predictions do notice in this passage?

How does it point forward to Jesus's victory?

When Christians partake in the Lord's Supper to remember and proclaim Jesus's death until He comes again (1 Corinthians 11:26), they also reflect on His resurrection and proclaim the fact that He lives.

Few of Jesus's words are as familiar as those He spoke at the Last Supper. According to the apostle Paul, Jesus then added, "Do this in remembrance of me" (1 Corinthians 11:24–25). Here, Jesus took the two Old Testament covenants from Sinai and Jeremiah and merged them together in His death and resurrection. Take a look.

*"This is the blood of the covenant that the LORD has
made with you concerning all these words."*

EXODUS 24:8

*"Look, the days are coming"—this is the LORD's declaration—"when I will
make a new covenant with the house of Israel and with the house of Judah."*

JEREMIAH 31:31

This covenant would be different because Jesus would be the sacrifice. Atonement would not be through the blood of bulls and goats but through Jesus's blood. Jesus's words at the Last Supper laid the groundwork for His disciples when they uncovered His empty tomb. They would be able to look back and understand that Jesus's death was not a disruption; rather, it was a message to proclaim about the kingdom of God. The words Jesus gave at the Last Supper—what we sometimes call the Words of Institution—redefined and re-empowered their mission, their proclamation, of a Messiah who in fact would save them.

Jesus's death and resurrection defeated our ultimate enemies: sin and death. Jesus's words provide the context for understanding the significance of the resurrection. All of Jesus's teaching leading up to His death and resurrection prepared His disciples (and us) to fully appreciate the point and scope of His ministry. Without Jesus's passion predictions, the disciples would have been very confused about the point of His ministry. His teaching about His death and resurrection frame those events as the consummation of God's redeeming work for all humanity. Those words in the upper room placed the final brick on a foundation Jesus had been laying for His disciples during His three years with them. And the conclusion pointed them to a ministry that would continue on in eternity (Matthew 26:29).

The risen Jesus told His disciples to go out and make disciples of all peoples. The commission was not limited to Israel: "But you will receive power when the Holy Spirit has come on you, and you will be my witnesses in Jerusalem, in all Judea and Samaria, and to the ends of the earth" (Acts 1:8). Jesus's predictions were not just for those first disciples—they are a proclamation to the entire world that Jesus is the One true Savior of all. It would be a redeeming, restorative, redemptive ministry that would affect the entire planet and, in the end, reverse and cure the negative consequences of humankind's sin and fall.

How does partaking in the Lord's Supper offer us the
opportunity to proclaim what Jesus predicted?

DAY 5

Jesus's Willingness to Endure Rejection Is the Key to Our Salvation

KEY SCRIPTURES
Psalm 118:22; Mark 8:31; 14:49; John 1:11-12

God treated Jesus as if He lived your life and mine, so He could treat you and me as if we lived the life of Jesus. That's the glorious gospel of grace. Sound too good to be true? If so, you are beginning to understand the concept of grace. Unimaginably, the price Jesus paid for our forgiveness through His victory on the cross included a life-long experience of rejection.

Consider the following Scriptures:

The stone that the builders rejected has become the cornerstone.

PSALM 118:22

[Jesus must] be rejected by the elders, chief priests, and scribes, be killed.

MARK 8:31

*"Every day I was among you, teaching in the temple,
and you didn't arrest me. But the Scriptures must be fulfilled."*

MARK 14:49

*He came to his own, and his own people did not receive him.
But to all who did receive him, he gave them the right to be
children of God, to those who believe in his name.*

JOHN 1:11-12

What comfort does Jesus's rejection give you in your struggles?

The Gospels report that no one in Jesus's family (with the exception of his mother, Mary) believed he was the long-awaited Messiah. We even learn that they were embarrassed by Him: "When his family heard this, they set out to restrain him, because they said, 'He's out of his mind'" (Mark 3:21). Family and friends in his hometown of Nazareth went so far as to be "offended by him" and asked, "Isn't this the carpenter, the son of Mary, and the brother of James, Joses, Judas, and Simon? And aren't his sisters here with us?" (Mark 6:3). And elsewhere we're told that "not even his brothers believed in him" (John 7:5). But it wasn't just Jesus's family that rejected Him, it was the religious elite who had studied the Scriptures and should've been most prepared to identify Jesus as the Messiah.

The religious leaders of Israel comprehensively rejected Jesus, fulfilling His predictions that He would suffer and be rejected "by the elders, chief priests, and the scribes" (Mark 8:31). (Elders were distinguished laymen and financial aristocracy; ruling priests filled the role of High Priest, like Caiaphas, and were usually from Sadducean background; and scribes were mostly Pharisees, such as Gamaliel.) A careful reading of the Gospels reveals the wording of Jesus's prediction matches the events of the narrative exactly. Jesus's passion predictions included His understanding that He would face the agony of death and sin alone. They cover the historical events as well as the internal thoughts and emotions of others. Only God can see inside the hearts of men with such precision.

Have you considered that Jesus endured a hopeless situation because of our hopeless condition? How does that shape your faith?

Read Romans 5:8.

But God proves his own love for us in that while we
were still sinners, Christ died for us.

ROMANS 5:8

The death and resurrection of Jesus included rejection so that you may never be rejected. Maybe this is an excellent opportunity for you to extend unconditional love to a friend or loved one. Thanks be to God for His grace and that we serve a God of many second chances.

As we conclude, wrap yourself again in the truth of God's love for you. Jesus knew He would endure rejection (Matthew 26:31) and even His closest friends would "fall away," and yet John reminds us, "he loved them to the end" (John 13:1)—which is to remind us of this key truth: Jesus loves us perfectly.

Jesus Rebuilds and Restores the Wrecks of My Life

Start

Welcome to Session 2 of Body of Proof.
Use this section to get the conversation started.

Over the past week your personal study has helped you see the importance of Jesus's predictions that He would rise from the dead on the third day.

> What was your most significant takeaway from the last group session or the week's personal study?

This week, we'll discover the powerful truth of Jesus's promise to rebuild the temple "in three days" (John 2:19) and learn what it means for Jesus to bring heaven and earth together in His resurrected body.

> What do you find most compelling about the resurrection of Jesus?

The resurrection of Jesus upended what it meant to be in a relationship with God. Instead of a temple people had to visit to make sacrifices and participate in rituals—all of which were good and necessary—we can now meet with God through Jesus. His resurrected body fulfills the role of the temple and makes His church the temple of the Holy Spirit. He compels us to bring hope to those around us in need of freedom from toil and effort-based attempts to please God.

Pray together before watching this week's video teaching.

Watch

Use this section to take notes and follow the video teaching.

Central Truths

Religion aways misses grace because "religion" misses Jesus.

God and humanity are now to meet perfectly and completely—
not in a temple, but in Jesus.

We are the people who bring hope.

Dominus Flevit, The Mount of Olives

Key Texts: Matthew 27:52; Luke 19:38-42; John 2:18–22

Dominus Flevit, which translates from Latin as "The Lord Wept," was fashioned in the shape of a teardrop to symbolize the tears of Christ. This space was built on a necropolis—a cemetery with over five hundred ossuaries (bone boxes), many of which have Christian iconography. This spot is resurrection ground (Matthew 27:52). The views of the Temple Mount are second-to-none.

For more on the Mount of Olives view the video at this QR Code.

For more on Jewish ossuaries view the video at this QR Code.

Discuss

Use this section to discuss the video teaching.

READ

The temple was the center of Jewish life because it was the place where heaven and earth met. When Jesus overturned the money changing tables in the temple, He rejected the hypocrisy and legalism and promised to provide a new future through His resurrection. In His death and resurrection, Jesus fulfilled all the temple was designed to provide. Through His death and resurrection, Jesus rebuilds and restores all the wrecks in my life.

Read John 2:13–22 together.

Why did Jesus drive out the money changers? What can we learn from His actions here?

What about Jesus's statements confused the religious elites?

How did Jesus fulfill the role of the temple and the sacrifices offered there?

APPLY

1. Jesus extends grace to all of us.

How was overturning the tables in the temple and act of mercy and grace?

How does Jesus provide us with something better than empty ritual and rule following?

Jeremiah said, "Religion misses grace because it misses Jesus." What did He mean by this?

2. The resurrection verified that everything Jesus said was true.

Reread John 2:22. How did the resurrection prove these statements of Jesus to be true?

3. Jesus has the power to rebuild the wrecks in our lives.

Just as Jesus rebuilt the temple, He can rebuild you. What part of your life and story most needs Jesus's resurrection power?

What are you following instead of Jesus that you need to turn away from and ask him to rebuild on a surer foundation?

CLOSE

Read Luke 19:38–42.

What led Jesus to weep over Jerusalem?

In one of the most heart-wrenching scenes in the Gospels, Luke records Jesus weeping over Jerusalem. We can sense the echo of Jesus's cry today as we take in the landscape of anxiety, despair, and depression around the world. *If you only knew what would bring you peace.*

Jesus wants us to have peace. The resurrection secures that peace for us. When we place our trust in God, He can give us peace even when we feel pressure.

Why should the resurrection provide us with peace?
How is it giving you peace?

Continuing in our personal study this week, we will see that we can trust the biblical account of the resurrection. Jesus consistently demonstrated and the Bible attests to His power to raise people from the dead. Jesus has resurrection power.

Close in prayer and remind the group to complete the five days of personal study.

I Can Trust the Resurrection Because:

Jesus has Resurrection Power

DAY 1

Jesus Demonstrated Resurrection Power

KEY SCRIPTURES
Matthew 9:18–26; Mark 5:21–43; Luke 8:40–56

What helps you believe in Jesus's power?

After reading about the resurrection of Jairus's daughter in today's key Scriptures, list the specific details you noticed in the account.

The Scriptures record nine resurrection miracles—three in the Old Testament; six in the New Testament, of which Jesus performed four. This week I emphasize these remarkable stories because it's probable that they influenced the way the followers of Jesus interpreted the Easter event. From our point of view, privileged with hindsight, we may see these miraculous resurrections as an foreshadowing of the resurrection of Jesus and of the future resurrection of His followers. But from the point of view of those who encountered the risen Jesus—with no well-established, uniform belief about resurrection before—the miraculous resurrections likely defined aspects of Jesus's resurrection. I don't see how it could have been otherwise. It's not coincidence that the same language is used in reference to those Jesus raised up as in reference to His resurrection.

Why do you suppose Scripture focuses on resurrection miracles?

The first Easter weekend is a historical event when, on the third day after Jesus's crucifixion, death was transformed into victory. Further, Jesus demonstrated His resurrection power in that, while others were reportedly raised only to die again, Jesus was raised immortally. Jesus authorized His disciples to preach the good news of the reign of God and, among other things, to "raise the dead" (Matthew 10:8).

In addition to these summary statements, the Gospels narrate three specific stories of people raised from the dead by Jesus. In one story, Jairus, the ruler of a synagogue, came to Jesus to ask Him to heal his daughter. She died only moments before Jesus arrived (Matthew 9:18–26; Mark 5:21–43; Luke 8:40–56). The story's details may suggest firsthand eyewitness testimony, from the desperation of the father and the sad report that reached Him—"Your daughter is dead. Why trouble the the teacher anymore?" (Mark 5:35)—to the mocking laughter in response to Jesus's words—"Why are you making a commotion and weeping? The child is not dead but asleep" (v. 39).

The details included point to eyewitness accounts. For example, the Aramaic words Jesus spoke to restore the girl: "'Talitha, koum'" (which is translated, 'Little girl, I say to you get up')" (v. 41). The appearance of the name Jairus, along with his identification with respect to the local synagogue (probably the one at Capernaum), points to the memory of this miraculous and specific episode in the ministry of Jesus.

What is the purpose of Jesus demonstrating His power to raise the dead?

How do the miracles of Jesus inform our theology and understanding of God and His intervention in our lives?

If we aren't careful, we may be attempted to read the New Testament records as another story or myth—like those found in novels or other religions—but the specificity of the New Testament accounts is intentional. They are historical events that happened in a particular place and time. Across the Gospels, the witnesses recorded Jesus's miraculous power to heal the sick, to control the natural world, forgive sins, and to raise the dead. One of the reasons we can trust that Jesus rose from the dead is that He clearly demonstrated the power to raise the dead. He laid down His life to take it up again (John 10:18). He alone is Master of life and death.

DAY 2

Resurrected Lives; Resurrected Hearts

KEY SCRIPTURES
Luke 7:11-17

When was the last time you were truly afraid?

Take time to contemplate a time the Lord came through in a situation of great adversity. What did you learn about Jesus through that experience?

In the first century world of Jesus, life expectancy was only twenty years, and people's final days often came with a great deal of suffering.[3] Skeletal remains suggest that as many as one quarter of the Roman Empire, on any given day, was sick, dying, or in need of immediate medical attention; often only one third of the skeletons found in archaeological digs from that time are those of adults (which emphasizes the mortality of children).[4] Infant mortality was as high as 25 percent, and most children wouldn't live past the age of ten.[5] As Bible students, we shouldn't miss that two of the three individuals Jesus raises from the dead were children.

How do knowing details like the ones you just read increase your faith in Jesus and His resurrection power?

In this second resurrection story, Jesus raised the only son of a widow (Luke 7:11–17). He encountered the funeral party as it left the village of Nain on its way to the place of burial. The boy died that day or perhaps the previous evening. Why do we know this is eyewitness testimony in Luke's Gospel? Several distinctive details were recalled, such as the name of the village; the woman being a widow; the deceased boy being her only son; Jesus touching the coffin; the stopping of the bearers; and the startling movement of the deceased, who is said to have "sat up" (v. 15).

> Why is reading the Bible with first century eyes important? (For example, when we understand life expectancy in the time of Jesus, we understand why His healing ministry was so widely received.)

These intentional details underscore the historicity and authenticity of these claims. Don't gloss over the fact that the Scriptures record the dead boy sat up. Can you imagine the elation (and shock) of all who were mourning—especially his mother, who was also a widow? God came through in the face of the greatest adversity.

As we learned last week, the Old Testament predicted and proclaimed Jesus's ministry. In this scene where He raised the son of a widow, Jesus revealed He had power similar to that of Elijah and Elisha (1 Kings 17:17–24; 2 King 4:18–37). In a first century world rooted in Jewish belief, this would lead the people to conclude that Jesus was indeed a prophet and that through His activity, God was visiting His people.

However, beyond a mere historical account and demonstration of power, these resurrection miracles have practical applications for our lives. This story also shows the lengths Jesus will go to meet people at their greatest points of need. Notice how our passage focused on the helplessness of the widow, deprived of the support of both her husband and her son. This draws attention to the gracious compassion of Jesus in caring for those in distress. So, it is not just Jesus's resurrection power that is available to us, but the heart of Christ who comforts the weak, afflicted, needy, and the spiritually dead. The same comfort and the same power is available to all who trust in Jesus.

> What comfort does this account offer you?

> Why should we always seek to find the practical application of these accounts?

DAY 3

Jesus Doesn't Shame Doubters, He Sharpens Us, Part I

KEY SCRIPTURES
Matthew 11:2–13; Luke 7:22

How you ever wrestled with doubts? How did you process them?

Doubt is not disbelief. There is a huge difference between doubt and disbelief. Eliminating doubt from life is impossible. As followers of Jesus, we must be prepared to process our doubts and help others process their doubts.

Even John the Baptist had doubts. Read Matthew 11:2-13 and Luke 7:22.

How should John the Baptist's doubts help us think about our own?

What distinguishes doubt from disbelief?

John the Baptist had already identified Jesus as the Messiah, but guess what? He needed some reassurance. If John the Baptist can doubt, so can we. The Gospel writers carefully recorded that the afterlife belief in bodily resurrection was not only among the pious or the eccentric of the day. Even Herod Antipas had heard about Jesus and later wondered if Jesus was the beheaded John the Baptist raised from the dead (Mark 6:16; Matthew 14:1–12; Luke 9:7–9).

But Jesus responded to John's doubt by providing evidence of resurrection miracles associated with His Messiahship. Looking at John the Baptist, it's important to note that doubt and disbelief aren't the same thing.

Consider it this way:

DOUBT says, "I **CAN'T** believe. Help me."

DISBELIEF says, "I **WON'T** believe. I don't want help."

Doubt is the enemy's weapon to lead us to disbelief. Did you know the devil only spoke three times in the entire Bible? Each time his goal was to cause people to doubt. The devil tempted Adam and Eve, Job, and finally, Jesus. When we experience adversity or isolation or suffering, the devil will attempt to get us to doubt what we know is true. John proclaimed Jesus as "the Lamb of God, who takes away the sin of the world" (John 1: 29), but he still doubted. Even so, look where he took his doubts: straight to Jesus (Matthew 11:2-3).

When we doubt, we should not hide from Jesus—He already knows. Like John the Baptist, let's take our doubts directly to Jesus. Notice also how John also involved his buddies when he doubted. Even though he was imprisoned, he still shared his doubts with friends. As growing Christians, we have to be committed to consistently surrounding ourselves with the people of God through a local church. Let's follow John the Baptist's example of doubting in community. We'll turn to Jesus's response to John the Baptist's doubts tomorrow.

Do you have a community of people—who are preferably further along than you—that you can share your doubts with, without fear of being condemned? What is the value in having these people in your life?

How does the resurrection of Jesus calm or answer your doubts?

DAY 4

Jesus Doesn't Shame Doubters, He Sharpens Us, Part II

KEY SCRIPTURES
Matthew 11:2–13; Luke 7:22; Jude 22–25

Describe Jesus's response to John the Baptist. What does this teach us about Jesus?

Jesus could have shamed John the Baptist for doubting. He could has said, "How could you doubt me after all that you've seen and heard? What kind of believer are you?" Jesus could have shunned John too: "Hey, just trust and believe. You don't really need to know the answer to your question." And that would have shattered him. Instead, Jesus sharpened him! Notice Jesus responded directly to John the Baptist's question with evidence, not emotion.

> *"Go and report to John what you hear and see: The blind receive their sight, the lame walk, those with leprosy are cleansed, the deaf hear, the dead are raised, and the poor are told the good news."*
>
> MATTHEW 11:4-5

Jesus reminds us that faith is not what we feel—faith is what we believe! Faith does not equal certainty; rather, faith equals trusting God through the uncertainty. His reply to the imprisoned John the Baptist, Jesus said, "the dead are raised" (Matthew 11:5; Luke 7:22).

Why did Jesus connect the resurrection of the dead to His identity as the Messiah?

Next, notice how Jesus affirmed John, "Truly I tell you, among those born of women no one greater than John the Baptist has appeared" (Matthew 11:11). Here's the application and passage payoff: God can use our doubts to propel us to a much stronger and sharper faith if we let Him. We can rest in the fact that Jesus will never shun us for doubting, but He also wants us to bring our doubts directly to Him.

Another immediate next step from today's Bible study should be a renewed commitment to surround ourselves with growing Christians. John's friends stood with him in his doubt. Curiosity is a hallmark of believers who love God with all their heart, soul, and mind. We need to be curious and doubt our doubts, not just our beliefs. A byproduct of being curious and thinking Christianly is that our questions will grow very quickly, which will stimulate conversation and grow our faith because Jesus is big enough to sustain our questions and answer our doubts. It does not require much effort to be curious. Being curious can also help other individuals doubt their doubts.

> What does it look like to doubt your doubts? Why should we be willing question our doubts as we often do our beliefs?

People are not all that stable—we are constantly changing and given to doubt. This is a human characteristic. Why do we take our doubts so seriously? We need to doubt them more, to test them further. We live in a world a lot like first-century Rome, a world that is growing increasingly secular. We need to do a better job disseminating good reasons for holding onto the Christian faith. Jude admonishes us to focus on strengthening the faith of our friends when they experience doubt:

> *Have mercy on those who waver; save others by snatching them from the fire; have mercy on others but with fear, hating even the garment defiled by the flesh. Now to him who is able to protect you from stumbling and to make you stand in the presence of his glory, without blemish and with great joy, to the only God our Savior, through Jesus Christ our Lord, be glory, majesty, power, and authority before all time, now and forever. Amen.*

> JUDE 22-25

> What are you facing right now that may be causing you to doubt? Which of these doubts might you question or seek the counsel of wise friends?

DAY 5

All Questions Won't Be Answered Here

KEY SCRIPTURES
Deuteronomy 29:29

How has your faith in the resurrection been build up over this week?

In the earliest days of Christianity an "apostle" was first and foremost a man who claimed to be an eyewitness of the Resurrection . . . to preach Christianity meant primarily to preach the Resurrection.[6]

C. S. LEWIS

"Never doubt in the dark what God showed you in the light," is a reminder my pastor, Dr. Jack Graham regularly shares with our congregation. Or sometimes he modifies it a bit, "Never trade what you do know for what you don't." These are great truths to live by, and they parallel the teaching of Moses:

The hidden things belong to the LORD our God, but the revealed things belong to us and our children forever, so that we may follow all the words of this law.

DEUTERONOMY 29:29

The Lord our God has secrets known to no one. The truth of this passage reminds us we are not accountable for the things we do not know, the things God has not revealed to us. But we are accountable for all that God has revealed to us. This is why the New Testament—its teaching, theology, and practical steps for Christian living—focuses on the resurrection of Jesus Christ.

A staggering three hundred verses in the New Testament address the resurrection across its 260 chapters.[7] Author Lee Strobel often says, "Every single shred of evidence for the resurrection of Jesus Christ is also evidence for my eventual resurrection."[8] And in a death-devastating promise, Jesus guarantees the believer's resurrection: "I am the resurrection and the life. The one who believes in me, even if he dies, will live" (John 11:25). In a radical comparison, Paul challenges

Christians, saying if the historical fact of Jesus's resurrection is false, they should "eat and drink, for tomorrow we die" (1 Corinthians 15:32). In other words, if Jesus didn't rise from the dead, we should live however we please with no margins or guardrails.

How is the resurrection of Jesus influencing your practical belief?

How is the resurrection of Jesus building your hope and trust in Him?

History tells us something happened to Jesus on that early Sunday morning—something that changed the lives of the people who witnessed it. (See Mark 16:14; Luke 24:34–43; John 20:19–31; and Acts 1:3–4; 9:3–6 for some post-resurrection appearances.) On Friday night, the day of the crucifixion, the disciples were running scared. A few days later they were more than willing to endure ridicule, imprisonment, mistreatment, and even death. And in the book of Acts, we see they told the Sanhedrin, "we are unable to stop speaking about what we have seen and heard" (Acts 4:20; see also 4:1–3,18–20). Jesus's resurrection power became real to them, and they boldly proclaimed their faith in it as a historical reality.

Christianity is quintessentially a resurrection religion. Without the resurrection of Jesus there is no Christianity. Yet practically, is it possible that just one morning could have changed the world? Could most, if not all, of life's problems be addressed by an unusual occurrence on a Sunday morning so long ago? Could it be that God's answer to the injustice in our world is exactly what came to us over a thirty-nine-hour period at a Jewish criminal's borrowed tomb in a Roman outpost? Could it be so simple? In a word, *yes*. This is the promise of God's glorious Word.

As we close this week's study, let's pause and thank God for what we do know: Jesus Christ is risen from the dead and we will rise with Him in glory (John 14:19)!

The Greatest
Comeback
of All Time

Start

Welcome to Session 3 of Body of Proof.
Use this section to get the conversation started.

Over the past week your personal study has helped you see the importance of Jesus's demonstrations of resurrection power and how that power applies to our lives through our own resurrection from sin and death.

> What was your most significant takeaway from the last group session or the week's personal study?

> When did you first "see" Jesus? In other words, share about a moment when Jesus became real to you.

Jesus's death by Roman crucifixion is the best established fact of the ancient world. If we can't believe Jesus of Nazareth died by Roman crucifixion, we can't believe anything about the ancient world. Our faith, and consequently our hope, is built on a solid and verifiable foundation. This week, we'll examine that foundation as we follow the final moments of Jesus's death and His victory over death in resurrection. Like Mary, we will see and believe (John 20:18). Standing at the traditional site of Jesus's tomb, we'll learn that seeing Jesus changes everything about our lives.

Pray together before watching this week's video teaching.

Watch

Use this section to take notes and follow the video teaching.

Central Truth

The day you see Jesus will be the best day of your life. Like Mary, you will exclaim, "I have seen the Lord!" (John 20:29). And that truth changes everything.

BODY *of* PROOF

Church of the Holy Sepulchre

Key Text: John 20:1-18

According to our best information scripturally and archaeologically, we believe the Church of the Holy Sepulchre complex to be the location of Jesus's crucifixion, tomb, and resurrection.

The Gospels agree that Jesus was buried in a known tomb belonging to Joseph of Arimathea (Matthew 27:57; Luke 23:50-51; John 19:38) and that after Jesus's burial, the entrance to the tomb was sealed with a stone.

The tomb was hewn from stone (Luke 23:53), and it was a new tomb (Matthew 27:60; John 19:41). The tomb was in a garden near the place where Jesus was crucified (John 19:41-42) and that the place of execution was "near the city" (John 19:20).

Additionally, it's clear that it was outside the walls of Jerusalem at the time because Jesus suffered "outside the gate" (Hebrews 13:12).

For more on the Church of the Holy Sepulchre view the video at this QR Code.

For more on Herod's family tomb view the video at this QR Code.

Discuss

Use this section to discuss the video teaching.

READ

Jesus Christ shattered the gates of death for us and now reins as our living Lord. He is alive. We are, right now, alive with Him (Colossians 3:1-4). In other words, our living hope is based on the historical, unchangeable fact of Jesus's physical, bodily resurrection from the dead.

Read John 20:1–18 together.

How did the disciples and Mary respond differently to what they found? How were their responses alike?

How did Jesus demonstrate specific care for Mary? What are some ways He provides the same kind of specific care to us?

APPLY

1. We have a living hope.

The Bible teaches us that in Christ we have a "living hope" (1 Peter 1:3), a "better hope" (Hebrews 7:19), and "sure" hope (Hebrews 6:19). What do these words describing our hope teach us about the kind of hope we have?

What about Christian hope makes it distinct from the hope other faiths or non-religious people have?

What is the relationship of hope to resurrection?

2. Our hope never disappoints.

What makes hope found outside of the resurrection fragile or incomplete?

How does the resurrection of Jesus equip you to face your struggles and disappointments differently? Share an example.

3. Without Christ there is no hope.

Why does the fact of the resurrection compel us to share our testimony about the resurrection?

How could you use your encounter with the risen Lord, like Mary, to share about the resurrection?

CLOSE

If you knew with certainty that you would live forever, what would you do differently? What risks would you take? Are you a believer who brings hope to those around you? As a believer, do you base your hope on your feelings or the objective facts of God's unchanging Word?

How would you answer those questions?

Who needs to hear about the hope you have in Jesus?

Continuing in our personal study this week, we will see that the resurrection historically verifiable and hope sustaining. Practically, we will also learn the resurrection also means that Christianity is the only faith will ultimately make sense of our suffering. The gospel's explanatory power with life's biggest questions supports its truthfulness.

Close in prayer and remind the group to complete the five days of personal study.

I Can Trust the Resurrection Because:

The Resurrection Makes Sense of Suffering

DAY 1

A Living Hope

KEY SCRIPTURES
1 Peter 1:3

Blessed be the God and Father of our Lord Jesus Christ. Because of his great mercy he has given us new birth into a living hope through the resurrection of Jesus Christ from the dead.

1 PETER 1:3

What does Peter mean when he calls our hope in Christ a "living hope"?

Jesus's bodily resurrection secures our present and future with a "living hope." In fact, the Bible teaches us that in Christ we have a "living hope" (1 Peter 1:3), a "better hope" (Heb 7:19), and "secure" hope (Heb 6:19). Indeed, this living hope is such that we must be prepared to defend and explain this hope when we are challenged by a hopeless world (1 Peter 3:15). C. S. Lewis defined hope this way:

> *Hope is one of the Theological virtues. This means that a continual looking forward to the eternal world is not (as some modern people think) a form of escapism or wishful thinking, but one of the things a Christian is meant to do. It does not mean that we are to leave the present world as it is. If you read history you will find that the Christians who did most for the present world were just those who thought most of the next.*[9]

Yet, we live in a society that has largely given in to despair, that's lost hope. And that leads to a lot of suffering and angst. Many people wonder *What is the point of life?* But the resurrection provides us with hope. Resurrection hope is what sustains us in suffering. According to Jesus, it gives us purpose. Which means your whole life can be poured out in a God-serving way. That's what the resurrection does for us. We are and continue to become the people who bring hope. Hope is only found in Christ, usually through a Christian used by God's Spirit to share the Word of God.

This first line of evidence from Paul helps us understand why we can have hope in the face of suffering:

I consider that the sufferings of this present time are not worth comparing with the glory that is to be revealed to us.

ROMANS 8:18

Hope in God, as much as faith in God, is the hallmark of our new life in Christ, "Through him you believe in God, who raised him from the dead and gave him glory, so that your faith and hope are in God" (1 Peter 1:21). As we trust in God, we must wrap ourselves in the truth that our hope stands: Jesus Christ shattered the gates of death for us and now reins as our living Lord. He is alive. As followers of Jesus we are "in Christ." In other words, our living hope is based on the, unchangeable fact of Jesus's, bodily resurrection from the dead. Because the end of His suffering was hope, the end of our suffering will also be hope. And this is not hope in hope, this is hope in a person, Jesus Christ, because He walked out of the grave alive!

How does the resurrection give you hope in hard circumstances?

If you knew with certainty that you would live forever, what would you do differently? What risks would you take? Are you a believer who brings hope to those around you? If so, how?

How does resurrection hope help you reconsider your suffering?

Hope calls us to action because hope endures. This hope will carry us through our most challenging moments. Our hope in Christ never disappoints. End today with this reminder.

This hope will not disappoint us, because God's love has been poured out in our hearts through the Holy Spirit who was given to us.

ROMANS 5:5

DAY 2

An Enduring Hope

KEY SCRIPTURES
Proverbs 4:18-19; Ephesians 2:12

The path of the righteous is like the light of dawn, shining brighter and brighter until midday. But the way of the wicked is like the darkest gloom; they don't know what makes them stumble.

PROVERBS 4:18-19

At that time you were without Christ, excluded from the citizenship of Israel, and foreigners to the covenants of promise, without hope and without God in the world.

EPHESIANS 2:12

The power that united the apostles, launched the first church, and invaded the Roman Empire was the certain knowledge and belief that Jesus had physically risen from the dead: "**With great power** the apostles continued to testify to the resurrection of the Lord Jesus. And God's grace was so powerfully at work in them all" (Acts 4:33 NIV, emphasis added).

Paul proclaimed that "[Jesus] was declared the Son of God **with power** . . . by the resurrection from the dead" (Romans 1:4 NASB, emphasis added). Paul's personal testimony and message explained that through the resurrection, Jesus demonstrated that He is completely unique. Jesus Christ has the power not only to lay down His life but also to take it up again (John 10:18).

Without the resurrection there would be no good news, and the New Testament would not even make sense. It's the foundation of our hope because it is the foundation of our faith.

How central is teaching on the resurrection in the church today:

1	2	3	4	5
Afterthought			Absolute Center	

Why did you choose this rating, and what can the church do to improve it?

As followers of Jesus, we live by faith in the tension between two resurrections: Jesus's first resurrection and ours. The bodily resurrection of Jesus guarantees our future bodily resurrection. This is why our hope is said to be both objective (like the kind of hope we discussed in yesterday's personal study) and subjective for the believer. Just as "faith" can be subjective (the act or state of believing) or objective (the content of belief), so "hope" can refer either to an anticipation (even a certainty) of good things to come or to the content of that anticipation, the good things themselves.[10]

The hope we have because of the resurrection of Jesus is an energizing hope that causes us to endure. Resurrection hope is also subjective in that, while being led of the Holy Spirit, all believers share in an attitude of expectancy of present blessings from God in this life and the next.

There is no hope outside of Jesus Christ. Paul reminds us of this in Ephesians 2:12, saying we were "without hope and without God in the world." Since the Christian life is resurrection-centric, followers of Jesus are called to share this truth to bring hope to a hopeless world. Bringing hope alleviates suffering and speaks uniquely to this world's suffering, and it endures because it extends beyond this world.

How can believing in the resurrection minister to those in pain?

Record the way you would honestly respond to Jesus, using one of the following prompts:

Yes, Lord, I believe You are the resurrection and the life and that I will live because ...

I am still struggling with the resurrection because ...

DAY 3

Hope in our Arabia Experiences

KEY SCRIPTURES
Galatians 1:11-20

The apostle Paul came to believe in the gospel of Jesus through the miraculous Damascus road experience. This came after Jesus's resurrection. Paul went from persecuting and killing Christians to loving Jesus because of the resurrection. Have you ever stopped to consider that Paul, unlike the other apostles, met Jesus after the resurrection and ascension? Jesus's disciples all met Jesus prior to His passion and resurrection; Paul knew Jesus as the resurrection—the same way we know Jesus today.

How did Paul come to this unshakable, unquenchable belief in Jesus and the resurrection? When did he receive this creed, this resurrection material that he passed on to the church of Corinth (1 Corinthians. 15:3-7)? And what difference does it make to our lives today? Those are the questions we will seek to answer here.

The villainous and psychotic Emperor Nero (who reigned AD 54–68) martyred the apostle Paul (and Peter) around AD 67. Nero's persecution of Christians began in AD 64. This is an important fact because Paul obviously would have completed all of his epistles prior to his martyrdom.

Paul was converted to Christianity about two years after the crucifixion and resurrection of Jesus. Paul visited Jerusalem three years after his conversion on the road to Damascus (Galatians 1:18). What was Paul doing for those three years? Paul first went first to Arabia and then to Damascus (v. 17) to spend time with God, most possibly in prayer, study, and meditation. He decided to go to God first rather than any human source (v. 16), even the other apostles.

> Take a moment to put yourself in Paul's shoes at that point
> in his life. Can you imagine how Paul felt? He had overseen
> Stephen's martyrdom and had persecuted Christians. Then he
> met the resurrected Jesus. Identify what kinds of emotions you
> would have had if you were Paul.

Paul ran to Arabia. For three years he wrestled with God, and like Jacob before him, who wrestled with God and was left with a limp (Genesis 32:24-32), God left Paul with a thorn in the flesh. Paul was alone with God for three years.

N. T. Wright has pointed out some unique parallels between Paul's Arabia experience and Elijah's retreat to Horeb to escape Jezebel. Just as Elijah went into the wilderness to die but was spiritually resurrected (1 Kings 19), Paul had a spiritual resurrection in Arabia. Like Elijah, Paul left Arabia and went into Damascus, where God, ahead of Paul, had instructed a Christian man named Ananias to care for him.

Perhaps, like Paul, you think you have done the unimaginable. Maybe you have regret for past actions or feel that you have failed. Many Christ followers still feel that God could never use them. And yet consider the flawed people in the Bible whom God used. The key point is that ironically, Paul, once killed Christians. God can use anyone who yields to Him. God used all of Paul's experiences and all of his sufferings prior to and after coming to Christ to build his and others' faith. Our stories do not define us, but they do provide ways for God to use us.

Do you need an Arabia experience with God—a time to spend alone with Him and seek His healing, direction, and purpose? Describe what this would look like for you.

End today's study by thanking God for your church and small group. Then pray in affirmation to the triune God, using the following as prayer starters.

Father, I believe that You ...

Jesus, You are my ...

Holy Spirit, I thank You for ...

DAY 4

Hope When All Seems Hopeless

KEY SCRIPTURES
1 Corinthians 15:12-58

Thanks to the resurrection of Jesus, Christians are promised that the best is yet to come. We are promised that death is only the beginning, not the end, and suffering is only temporary. That is why the apostle Paul told the Thessalonian Christians who had lost their believing loved ones that though we grieve, we do not grieve like those who have no hope, because we know it is only a short interlude until we see them again (1 Thessalonians 4:13). But there is more. In the same passage Paul answered at least three vital questions that give us hope now and in the future.

1. What will the resurrection be like?

Read 1 Corinthians 15:51-52.

Cosmic signs and miracles will hasten the resurrection of the dead. The dead will rise suddenly. Loud noises will accompany this apocalyptic hastening of the dead. In 1 Thessalonians Paul stated that three different sounds will be heard at the resurrection: the cry or command of the Lord Himself, the voice of an archangel, and the trumpet of God (4:16).

2. What kind of resurrection body can we expect?

Read 1 Corinthians 15:35-44,50-56.

Our resurrection body will be a literal, physical body, not a spirit-ghost or apparition—we will look like Jesus (Philippians 3:21). Christ was raised in a physical body and Scripture tells us that our resurrection bodies will be patterned after His body (Luke 24:39).

Paul used two descriptive words to characterize resurrection life in verse 53: incorruptible (a body that never needs to be upgraded) and immortality (a body that will never die).

It is difficult to watch our bodies break down, but as believers, we hope because we know death is not the end. That doesn't mean we look forward to death, but as Pastor Greg Laurie shared on social media, "Only those who are prepared to die are really ready to live."[11]

3. Why does the resurrection matter for Us today?

Read 1 Corinthians 15:30-34,57-58.

Paul said if the resurrection never happened, the early Christians may as well stop suffering for Christ and dedicate their lives to pleasure (1 Corinthians 15:30-32). However, because Jesus has been raised, Paul stated that Christians should pursue holy living (vv. 33-34). From the beginning Christianity has taught the resurrection was not something to be embarrassed about but something to proclaim and, if necessary, to sacrifice our lives for.

The resurrection not only shapes our future but also energizes our present usefulness and ministry for the kingdom of God. Paul concluded this teaching with a powerful point in verse 58: What happens in the future with your resurrection body affects everything you do for God today. That is why Paul used the present tense, "Your labor in the Lord is not in vain," rather than the future tense, "Your labor will not be in vain." He was challenging believers never to give up, never to quit, but to "be steadfast, immovable, always excelling in the Lord's work."

We should never lack motivation to serve God with all our heart because we know everything we do for God will last for all eternity. Any suffering we endure for Jesus's sake will be worth it when we see Him and are welcomed into His eternal kingdom.

Christians can be as solid as a rock—steadfast and immovable—because the worst enemy, death, is defeated, and we have nothing to fear. We need to be strong. The resurrection promises us that our lives have eternal significance when devoted to our ever-living, resurrected Lord.

How is your faith in the resurrection making a tangible difference in the way you live and deal with suffering and hardship?

DAY 5

Nothing we Endure Compares to All that Is Ours in Christ

KEY SCRIPTURES

Acts 4:13-20

On Good Friday night, the day of the crucifixion, the disciples were running scared. A few days later they were more than willing to endure ridicule, imprisonment, mistreatment, and even death.

As we have learned in this Bible study, that Jesus Christ rose from the dead is an empirical claim. Christianity is unique from other religions in that you can test the claims and beliefs because they are falsifiable and verifiable. We can trust in the resurrection of Jesus because of—not in spite of—the evidence. The late non-Christian philosopher of religion Antony Flew said, "The evidence for the resurrection is better than for claimed miracles in any other religion. It's outstandingly different in quality and quantity."[12]

In the Greco-Roman world, death meant the end. There was no hope, only sorrow. The miracles performed in Jesus's name after His resurrection drew many converts. But it was the resurrection and what it meant for humanity that the Roman world found especially compelling. This is why Jesus's ministry was completely remarkable. He not only predicted His own death and bodily resurrection (Mark 9:31), but he charged His disciples to preach the kingdom of God and to "raise the dead" (Matthew 10:8). No wonder in the Gospels we read about large crowds following Jesus.

What message of Jesus makes Him most compelling to you?

It's not hard to imagine why the early Christian movement spread so rapidly around the Mediterranean world. Jesus's disciples were passionate eyewitnesses to the abundant life and resurrected body He promised. Peter and John said, "we are unable to stop speaking about what we have seen and heard" (Acts 4:20).

Most Romans had no confidence in an afterlife—none that we know of believed in resurrection. Even in mythology, stories of a return to life were rare and did not reflect beliefs with respect to mortals. A common motto found on epitaphs in Roman late antiquity reads: "I was not, I was, I am not, I care not."[13] If nothing else, it is an expression of hopelessness. But the resurrection of Jesus changed everything. With His resurrection the promise of an authentic, verified afterlife for the followers of Jesus gained a whole new degree of gravitas. What Jesus offered was not pie in the sky but a promise grounded in a real event— an event witnessed firsthand by several witnesses, not all friendly.

But the mockery, misrepresentations, caricatures, persecutions, and occasional martyrdoms could not stop the Christian movement. Its message of a loving God, the example of a loving community, in which every man, woman, and child was wanted and valued, and the hope of life in this world and beyond, thanks to the resurrection of Jesus, were irresistible. Many mocked but far more believed. They believed because they discovered that the gospel "is the power of God for salvation" (Romans 1:16). That power of God is available to every man, woman, and child who will turn from their sins and trust in Jesus. The resurrection is for all who believe in the gospel that saves.

What hope has this study given you in the resurrection?

How are you being challenged to make a rooted belief in the resurrection more central to your faith?

What passage of Scripture from this week has been most helpful?

We're All Traveling the Road to Emmaus

Start

Welcome to Session 4 of Body of Proof.
Use this section to get the conversation started.

This past week you learned an important truth that is immediately practical to our Christian lives: the resurrection makes sense of our suffering. This week, we will focus on the hope we have in experiencing Christ.

> What was your most significant takeaway from the last group session or the week's personal study?

> What are some ways Jesus has met you along the road of life?

In our closing session, we'll walk the actual first-century Emmaus road together with the prayer that our hearts burn within us, just like Cleopas and his friend, who experienced the risen Christ. Without the resurrection there would be no good news, and the New Testament would not even make sense. But Jesus has risen from the dead, and we have unending hope.

Pray together before watching this week's video teaching.

Watch

Use this section to take notes and follow the video teaching.

Central Truth

The power that united the apostles, launched the first church, and invaded the Roman Empire was the certain knowledge and belief that Jesus had physically risen from the dead.

The Road to Emmaus

Key Text: Luke 24:13-35

Luke writes about the Emmaus road in chapter 24 of his Gospel. Emmaus was a village in Judea and two disciples of Jesus were walking there, when the resurrected Christ joined them. Likely they were returning home after the Passover festivities since the Sabbath was over.

Were told they are "About seven miles from Jerusalem." "Seven miles" is literally sixty stadia from Jerusalem. A stadion is about 607 feet; therefore the distance is approximately 6.8 miles.

We can trust in the authenticity of this account and the cylindrical Roman mile markers and first-century road curbing remain to this day.

For more on Roman Milestones view the video at this QR Code.

For more about first-century tombs view the video at this QR Code.

Discuss

Use this section to discuss the video teaching.

READ

In the Gospel of Luke, Jesus's disciples are said to have lost all hope following the crucifixion. They gave up, and why wouldn't they? In that gripping scene in Luke 24:13-35, two disciples on the Emmaus road encountered an interesting stranger. Not realizing they were walking and conversing with the resurrected Messiah, they admitted, "we were hoping that he was the one" (Luke 24:21). The early Christian movement should have died out, but instead it thrived. Why? The resurrection of Jesus.

Read Luke 24:13-35 together.

How would you summarize the concerns on the minds of Cleopas and the other disciple?

Have you ever felt the way they felt? How do you personally relate to this passage?

APPLY

1. We hope in times of "seeming" hopelessness.

Jesus encountered the Emmaus disciples at a low point. What low points in your life has Jesus faithfully led you out of?

Our culture is plagued with hopelessness. How does the resurrection uniquely address such hopelessness?

2. We hope in fellowship.

Jesus ate with these disciples, and one day we will feast with Jesus in community in heaven. How does the resurrection create Christian community and fill it with meaning?

3. We hope in the promises of Scripture.

Jesus appealed to the prophets to verify His own resurrection.
What confidence can we have to do the same?

The promises of Scripture are resurrection promises.
Which are you trusting in today?

4. We hope forevermore in Jesus.

Name one concrete way that you are trusting Jesus for your future.

CLOSE

End the study knowing this: Because Jesus is raised, we will be raised with Him.
Jesus Christ has the power not only to lay down His life but also to take it up again
(John 10:18). More than two dozen times in the New Testament, followers of Jesus
are promised they will be raised with Jesus. No other promise occurs with more
frequency than the assurances of the believer's resurrection because it's linked
with Jesus's personal resurrection.

What hope does this promise give you today?

Share one key takeaway from this study.

Our personal study this week is a good one, so be sure to press in and complete
it! We end where we have focused our time in this study—the resurrection is the
foundation of our hope.

Close in prayer and remind the group to complete the five days of personal study.

I Can Trust the
Resurrection Because:

The Resurrection is the Foundation of our Hope

DAY 1

What the Bible Says about the Death of a Christian

KEY SCRIPTURES
Psalm 116:15

Hope, at times, can feel fragile. No more so than when we deal with death, but Christians can face death with hope. The Bible says so many wonderful things about the death of a Christian. Perhaps none more so than this:

The death of his faithful ones is valuable in the Lord's sight.

PSALM 116:15

Why would the death of a saint (anyone who believes in Jesus) be "valuable" to the Lord?

Once a person comes to know Jesus Christ through an act of faith, receiving the forgiveness of sin He so bountifully offers, there's not one sin a believer can commit that will keep him or her out of heaven. In Romans 8:35–39, we read:

Who can separate us from the love of Christ? Can affliction or distress or persecution or famine or nakedness or danger or sword? As it is written: Because of you we are being put to death all day long; we are counted as sheep to be slaughtered. No, in all these things we are more than conquerors through him who loved us. For I am persuaded that neither death nor life, nor angels nor rulers, nor things present nor things to come, nor powers, nor height nor depth, nor any other created thing will be able to separate us from the love of God that is in Christ Jesus our Lord.

ROMANS 8:35–39

How do verses like this encourage your faith and build your hope?

On the authority of God's Word, we can say that right now our loved ones who died following Christ are in His presence in heaven. But how can we be so sure? Second Corinthians tells us that to be absent from the body is to be present with the Lord (5:8). And on the cross, Jesus looked at the thief dying next to Him—the one who had expressed faith in Him—and said, "Truly I tell you, today you will be with me in paradise" (Luke 23:43).

Just before his death, the great preacher Dr. F. B. Meyer wrote these words to a close friend: "I have just heard, to my great surprise, that I have but a few days to live. It may be that before this reaches you, I shall have entered the palace. Don't trouble to write. We shall meet in the morning."[14] And Dr. William Carey, the great father of modern missions, wrote in his biography, "When I am gone, say nothing about Dr. Carey. Speak about Dr. Carey's Savior."[15]

For the believer, death means entering immediately into the glorious presence of Christ. But we must not think that all the past blessings with our loved ones are gone when their death comes. No, the memories linger, and more than that, the person who listens to the gospel, repents of sin, and turns to Christ in personal trust lives beyond physical death. Indeed, many of us have had to muster up those words "Goodbye for now." But under much better circumstances, we can say "Good morning" when we're called to see Jesus and our loved ones face-to-face. How can this be? Who gives victory over death? Who makes it possible for our sins to be forgiven? Who takes away the power of evil and grants life everlasting? The answer is this: God's Son and our Savior, the Lord Jesus Christ.

How does the resurrection allow us to face death with hope?

When have you seen believers demonstrate this belief? What can you learn from them?

DAY 2

A Hope and Life that Never Dies

KEY SCRIPTURES
John 11:25-26

Jesus said to her, "I am the resurrection and the life. The one who believes in me, even if he dies, will live. Everyone who lives and believes in me will never die. Do you believe this?"

JOHN 11:25-26

Jesus claims to be the resurrection *and* the life. How are these two ideas connected?

As we saw and learned in week one of our study, the background to this statement was the death of Lazarus, a dear friend of Jesus Christ. Lazarus and his two sisters, Martha and Mary, lived in the small village of Bethany, which is about two miles from Jerusalem and situated on the eastern slopes of the Mount of Olives. Bethany was a serene country setting. The villagers worked hard and long in the vegetable and grain fields of the valleys in that vicinity.

Lazarus and his sisters were all devout believers in the Lord. They saw in Jesus the promised Messiah whose life and ministry had been so clearly prophesied in the Jewish Scriptures. When Jesus came to Jerusalem, they offered Him a place to live and food at their home. But on the occasion of the narrative of our text, this lovely scene had turned into a tragic one with great grief.

Lazarus, Jesus's beloved friend, had suddenly gotten sick and died. Although messengers had sent for Jesus, four days passed between the death and burial of Lazarus and Jesus's arrival. The sisters knew Jesus had the power to heal the sick, and they had hoped he would make it to their house in time to heal their brother.

But it was too late. Lazarus was dead. He'd been buried for four days. For the time being, it was a hopeless scene. And amid their grief, both Martha and Mary had forgotten that Jesus not only healed the sick but also raised the dead. So when Jesus arrived, though He met Martha and Mary at separate times, they each said to Him, "Lord, if you had been here, my brother wouldn't have died" (John 11:21,32).

Verses 33 and 34 tell us, "When Jesus saw [Mary] crying, and the Jews who had come with her crying, he was deeply moved in his spirit and troubled. 'Where have you put him?' he asked. 'Lord,' they told him, 'come and see.'" This is the juncture where we read one of the shortest verses in all the Bible: "Jesus wept" (v. 35).

Yet earlier, in response to the sisters' sorrowful statements, Jesus was already turning their hopelessness back to hopefulness by reminding them that He is the resurrection and the life. As we shall see in our remaining studies this week, the same Scripture passage reassures us that Jesus continues to be:

- The Person of Hope

- The Power of Hope

- The Prerequisite of Hope

- The Promise of Hope

- The Permanence of Hope

Which of these is most intriguing to you?

What are some ways you've already seen Jesus to be some of these things?

What is one way your belief in Jesus is shaping your hope right now?

DAY 3

The Person and Power of Hope

KEY SCRIPTURES
John 11:25-26

The Person of Hope: "I Am"

Throughout the Gospel of John Jesus made seven "I am" statements. Making these statements, Jesus intentionally used the title of the eternal and self-existent God revealed throughout the Bible. This is the title God gave to Moses at the burning bush (Exodus 3:14), and it the Hebrew word for "He is" or "He exists."

The God of the Bible, the God of the patriarchs Abraham, Isaac, and Jacob, has no name like the other gods of antiquity. He is simply "I am." The One who is—the foundation of all being, the Creator and Sustainer of life. The uniqueness of God, the fact that there is no other god, means God has no need for a "name" that distinguishes Him from other the gods. He simply is, and He alone is the source of our hope.

How does it shift your perspective to see hope is knowable and personal?

The Power of Hope: "I Am The Resurrection"

The power that spoke the universe into existence is Jesus Christ. He is the power that caused the blind to see, the lame to walk, the deaf to hear, the mute to talk, the dead to live, the storms to calm. The power of Jesus Christ is dedicated to our deliverance, forgiveness, and salvation. The gospel of Jesus Christ "is the power of God for [the] salvation" of all who believe (Romans 1:16). Jesus promised that because He lives we will also live (John 14:19). This is our hope—Jesus Christ will freely forgive our sins and we will live with Him in heaven for all eternity.

Do you connect Jesus's power to His resurrection as the Scriptures do? What practical help and hope do we have as Christians when we do?

The Prerequisite of Hope: "Do You Believe This?"

Many things in life are unattainable, but we can all believe in Christ. These are key Scriptures that tell us so:

> *But to all who did receive him, he gave them the right to be children of God, to those who believe in his name.*
>
> JOHN 1:12

> *Believe in the Lord Jesus, and you will be saved—you and your household.*
>
> ACTS 16:31

> *Truly I tell you, anyone who hears my word and believes him who sent me has eternal life and will not come under judgment but has passed from death to life.*
>
> JOHN 5:24

> *If you confess with your mouth, "Jesus is Lord," and believe in your heart that God raised him from the dead, you will be saved. One believes with the heart, resulting in righteousness, and one confesses with the mouth, resulting in salvation.*
>
> ROMANS 10:9–10

Faith isn't complicated. Faith is a decision based on evidence. Again, have you placed your trust in Jesus Christ? Have you had a moment when you made a conscious, willful decision to turn to Him? If not, will you do that right now?

Why should the truth about the resurrection compel us to ask those around us the same question Jesus asked Mary and Martha? Who do you need to ask?

DAY 4

The Promise of Hope

KEY SCRIPTURES
John 11:25-26,43-44

The Promise of Hope: "He Shall Live"

The great promise of the resurrection is that in the same moment we take our last breath on earth, we are in face-to-face communion with our Lord: to be away from the body [is to be] at home with the Lord" (2 Corinthians 5:8). Salvation is a free gift from God (Romans 6:23), and we find that gift in full when we pass from this life to the next. The words that came from the lips of Jesus Christ Himself ring true in our hearts: "The one who believes in me, even if he dies, will live" (John 11:25).

How often does the thought that you will live forever with Jesus cross your mind? How could dwelling on that change your outlook?

Jesus set out to show His power over death, sin, and Satan, whether through resurrection or resuscitation, again and again. In the story we've been studying, Lazarus had been dead for four days (v. 43), yet when Jesus called His name, the man who had died came out of the grave (v. 44). In Jesus, the physically and spiritually dead will live again.

What was dead in you that Jesus called back to life?

The Permanence of Hope: "Shall Never Die"

Beyond the miracle of raising Lazarus from the dead physically, Jesus's promise that those who believe in Him will never die spiritually extends to us today. When we make a choice to place our trust in Jesus Christ, the eternal person of God comes to live inside our spirit, guaranteeing that we will live eternally with Him. When death comes to our door, it can take only the body, not the soul. And because Jesus Christ is the resurrection, we have the guarantee that we will be resurrected with a new heavenly body someday—a body that will never grow tired, old, or see decay. We're even promised there will be no more tears (Revelation 21:4).

How do these promises to have full life and never die work together?

Once more, the important question for today is this: Have you received Jesus Christ? You're not a Christian because you go to church, or because you're a good person, or because you've kept the Golden Rule. Being a Christian is all about being forgiven by the grace of God. In Jesus Christ we find forgiveness for sin, peace with God, and eternal resurrection life. Salvation is conditioned solely on faith in the New Testament. Works-based salvation is a grace-killer. The only thing you can bring to the cross has already been brought there: your sins. Have you placed your trust in Jesus Christ for your forgiveness of sin and eternal life with Him? You can do that right now. Trust in Christ.

If you haven't confesses faith in Jesus Christ, I invite you to do so right now.

If you have placed your faith in Jesus, spend a few moments thanking God for all that He has done for you.

DAY 5

Passing on the Creed of Hope

KEY SCRIPTURES

1 Corinthians 15:3-7

The resurrection narrative is found in all four Gospels and the book of Acts (Matthew 27:62–28:20; Mark 16; Luke 24; John 20–21; Acts 1:1-12). Therefore, if you ask Christians where to find the best evidence for Jesus's resurrection, most poeple will point you to the Gospels. The Gospel writers are excellent sources, but they are not the earliest sources for the resurrection of Jesus.

The apostle Paul is our best and earliest source for understanding when Christians came to believe in the bodily resurrection of Jesus. Paul also detailed reasons we can have hope for our own limitless resurrection bodies. In 1 Corinthians 15, Paul passed on the most important and earliest Christian creed, which is a formal statement of Christian beliefs. He said:

> *For I passed on to you as most important what I also received: that Christ died for our sins according to the Scriptures, that he was buried, that he was raised on the third day according to the Scriptures, and that he appeared to Cephas, then to the Twelve. Then he appeared to over five hundred brothers and sisters at one time; most of them are still alive, but some have fallen asleep. Then he appeared to James, then to all the apostles.*

1 CORINTHIANS 15:3-7

Based on this Scripture what do Christians believe about the resurrection?

What creeds (more broadly defined, perhaps a mission statement or set of values) does your church or small group have?

The source material for this creed is the oldest in the New Testament. It stretches back to within weeks of the resurrection event itself. The scholar James Dunn is "entirely confident" in stating that the tradition behind the composition of 1 Corinthians 15:3-4 was "formulated . . . within months of Jesus's death."[16]

Why do you think the Corinthians needed to be reminded of basic facts about the gospel? Why do we?

These early creeds preserved the Christian faith before the New Testament was written. The very first Christian generation did not have a Bible as we know it today. Therefore, these early creeds and hymns were extremely important in teaching the basics of the faith.

Paul didn't invent this creed. How do we know that? He said, "I passed on to you as most important what I also received" (v. 3). Paul was passing on a tradition that predates his letter to the Corinthian church—what early Christians came to believe about the resurrection and also when they believed it. Paul received it from Peter, James, and John (Galatians 1:18-20).

Paul passed it on because Christian faith is meant to be passed on. The resurrection isn't something for us to merely ingest all the facts about and hold on to ourselves; it is to be shared. Creeds are repeated and shared because they distill the essentials of a faith into a memorable few words.

There's better way for us to end a study on the hope we have in the resurrection today than by committing to do as Paul did and passing on the hope of the resurrection to those who need it.

What is your most significant takeaway from our four weeks together studying the resurrection?

Who in your life needs the hope that you have? End the study praying for them, and plan to share the hope of the resurrection with them in the coming days.

Sources

1. A.T. Robertson, Word Pictures in the New Testament (Nashville, TN: Broadman Press, 1933), Lk 24:27.
2. Jeremiah J. Johnston, The Resurrection of Jesus in the Gospel of Peter (New York and London: Bloomsbury T & T Clark, 2016), 103.
3. Jeremiah J. Johnston and Steve Green, Unimaginable: What Our World Would Be like without Christianity (Grand Rapids, MI: Bethany House, 2017).
4. Jeremiah J. Johnston, Unanswered: Lasting Truth for Trending Questions (New Kensington, PA: Whitaker House, 2015), p. 73.
5. "The Roman Empire: In the First Century. The Roman Empire. Life in Roman Times. Family Life," PBS, 2006, https://www.pbs.org/empires/romans/empire/family.html.
6. C. S. Lewis, Miracles (New York: Touchstone, 1996), 188-191.
7. Gary Habermas's article "Resurrection" in The Encyclopedia of Christian Civilization, First Edition. Edited by George Thomas Kurian. 2011 Blackwell Publishing Ltd. Published 2011 by Blackwell Publishing Ltd, page 1.
8. Lee Strobel, God's Outrageous Claims: Thirteen Discoveries That Can Transform Your Life (Grand Rapids, MI: Zondervan, 2005), 204.
9. C. S. Lewis, Mere Christianity (New York: HarperCollins, 2001), 134.
10. J. Ramsey Michaels, 1 Peter, vol. 49 of Word Biblical Commentary (Dallas: Word, Incorporated, 1988), 19.
11. Greg Laurie, "Only those who are prepared to die are truly ready to live," Facebook, July 28, 2017, https://www.facebook.com/watch/?v=10155453232301698
12. Gary Habermas, "My Pilgrimage from Atheism to Theism: An Exclusive Interview with Former British Atheist Professor Antony Flew." Available from the website of Biola University at www.biola.edu/antonyflew. See also Gary R. Habermas, Antony Flew, David J. Baggett (2009). "Did the Resurrection Happen?: A Conversation with Gary Habermas and Antony Flew" (Downers Grove, IL: InterVarsity Press), 85.
13. Frank Frost Abbott, The Common People of Ancient Rome (New York: Charles Scribner's Sons, 1911), 90.
14. F. B. Meyer, Bible.org, https://bible.org/illustration/f-b-meyer#:~:text=A%20few%20days%20before%20his%20death%2C%20Dr.%20F.,reaches%20you%2C%20I%20shall%20have%20entered%20the%20palace.
15. Timothy George, "The Lasting Contributions of a Wretched Worm," Christian History Institute, 1992, https://christianhistoryinstitute.org/magazine/article/lasting-contributions-of-a-wretched-worm.
16. James D. G. Dunn, Jesus Remembered. Christianity in the Making, vol. 1 (Grand Rapids: Eerdmans, 2003), 855.

JESUS IS RISEN INDEED!

THIS FACT CHANGES EVERYTHING!

Christianity's most important historical fact—the resurrection—is often misunderstood, creating a powerless Christianity. In *Body of Proof*, acclaimed apologist and scholar Dr. Jeremiah Johnston sets out to show why Jesus' victory over death is central to a believer's faith. Straightforward, accessible, and practical, this book examines the latest archaeological and textual findings and presents **seven tangible, fresh reasons to believe Jesus really rose from the dead—and why it matters today** as the foundation of our hope in the face of suffering and grief.

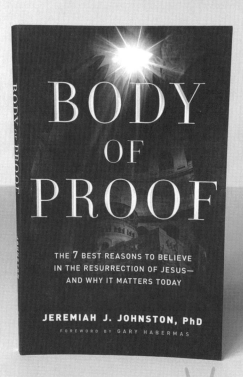

BODY OF PROOF

THE **7** BEST REASONS TO BELIEVE IN THE RESURRECTION OF JESUS— AND WHY IT MATTERS TODAY

JEREMIAH J. JOHNSTON, PhD

FOREWORD BY GARY HABERMAS

UNDERSTANDING THE IMPLICATIONS OF THE RESURRECTION WILL REVEAL THE POWER OF CHRIST IN YOU.

Jeremiah J. Johnston, PhD, Middlesex/Oxford, (www.christianthinkers.com) is a New Testament scholar and ministers internationally as president of Christian Thinkers Society. Jeremiah loves the local church, and also serves as pastor of apologetics and cultural engagement at Prestonwood Baptist Church and dean of spiritual development at Prestonwood Christian Academy.

PURCHASE YOUR COPY WHEREVER BOOKS ARE SOLD!

BETHANY HOUSE

a division of Baker Publishing Group

If only Solomon had written a book on wisdom.

Oh, wait.

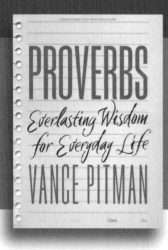

PROVERBS
Everlasting Wisdom for Everyday Life
VANCE PITMAN

Take a month-long journey through all 31 chapters of Proverbs. You'll not only gain an appreciation for this popular and applicable book of the Bible, you'll also begin to develop a daily habit of seeking wisdom from God's Word. In addition to the four session videos, you get access to 31 short, daily teaching videos (one for each chapter), all included in the purchase price of the *Bible Study Book*.

Learn more online or call 800.458.2772.
lifeway.com/proverbs

Lifeway

Step into God's beautiful story.

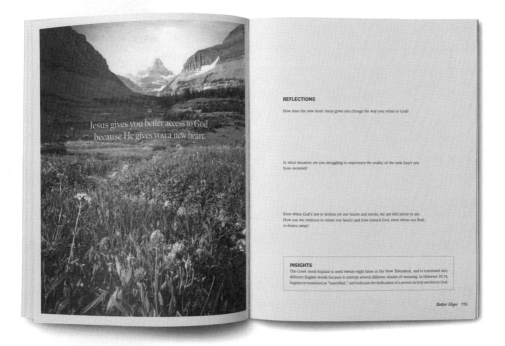

Storyteller is a Bible study series uniquely designed to be inviting, intuitive, and interactive. Each volume examines a key theme or story in a book of the Bible. Every week includes five days of short Scripture reading, a daily thought explaining each passage, a short list of questions for a group Bible study, and space for you to write down your discoveries. And new volumes are being added every year.

Learn more online or call 800.458.2772.
lifeway.com/storyteller

What a weekend!

Little did anyone know that the first Easter weekend would include the execution of Jesus, an earthquake, daytime darkness, an uprising, and a miracle unlike any the world had ever seen.

The event of the resurrection is what gives us hope and confidence in our salvation.

• Understand why you can accept the resurrection of Jesus.

• See the power that Jesus holds over life and death.

• Discover the resurrection's power to transform lives.

Studying on your own?
To enrich your study experience, be sure to access the videos available through a redemption code printed in this Bible Study Book.

Leading a group?
Each group member will need a Body of Proof Bible Study Book, which includes video access. This gives participants complete access to the video content individually.

ADDITIONAL RESOURCES

eBOOK
Includes the content of this printed book but offers the convenience and flexibility that come with mobile technology.

005847277 **$16.99**

DVD Set
005847284 **$29.99**

Price and availability subject to change without notice.